Top-Notch TISSUE BOX COVERS

Look What You Can Make!

This collection of tissue box covers in 7- and 10-mesh plastic canvas offers styles to fit any room or mood. Stitch a mix of fruits and vegetables for the kitchen. Spread Christmas cheer with a jolly Santa. Send a spinnaker sailing out to sea! You can create colorful pinwheels, bright bargello, 1940s flamingos—fourteen fanciful designs in all. They're great for gifts or to use in your own home-sweet-home!

About The Designer

Conn Baker Gibney was a prolific designer, artist, and crafter. The Ohio native lived and worked in New York for many years while adding his talents to the arts and crafts industry. He created hundreds of popular needlework designs, including these popular tissue box covers. They are reflections of the late Mr. Gibney's kind spirit and delightful sense of whimsy.

Table Of Contents

Spinnaker	2
Pinwheels	4
Forties Flamingos	6
Home Sweet Home	8
Blue Waves	11
Lightning	13
Tulips	15
Argyle	18
Mushrooms	20
Hearts	22
Zebra	23
Santa	24
Kitchen	25
Geometric	26

LEISURE ARTS, INC.
Little Rock, Arkansas

Spinnaker Boutique Tissue Box Cover

Size
4 1/2"w x 5 1/2"h x 4 1/2"d
(fits a 4 1/4"w x 5 1/4"h x 4 1/4"d boutique tissue box)

Supplies
Two 10 1/2" x 13 1/2" sheets of 7 mesh plastic canvas
Worsted weight yarn
Embroidery floss
#16 tapestry needle

Stitches Used
Backstitch, Gobelin Stitch, Overcast Stitch, and Tent Stitch. Refer to **General Instructions**, pages 28-31, for stitch diagrams.

Instructions
Follow charts to cut and stitch tissue box cover pieces. Use matching color Overcast Stitches for all joining. Matching long edges, join Sides. Join Top to Sides. For each Sail, match ♥'s, ★'s, and ◆'s; tack corners to Side #1.

Color Key	
╱	white
╱	yellow
╱	red
╱	lt blue
╱	dk blue
╱	green
╱	red (use 2 plies)
╱	white embroidery floss (use 6 strands)
╱	black embroidery floss (use 2 strands)
╱	metallic silver embroidery floss (use 6 strands)

www.leisurearts.com

Sail (24 x 28 threads) (stitch 2)

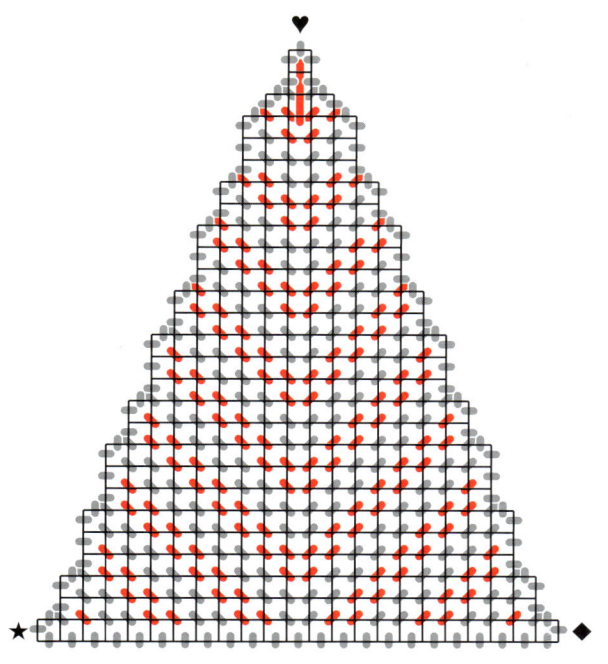

Top (32 x 32 threads)

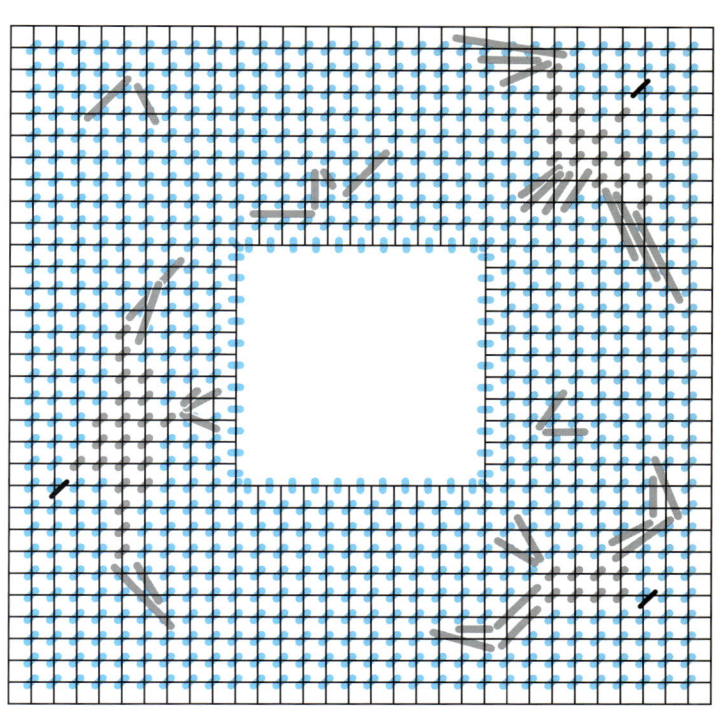

Side #1 (32 x 38 threads) (stitch 2)

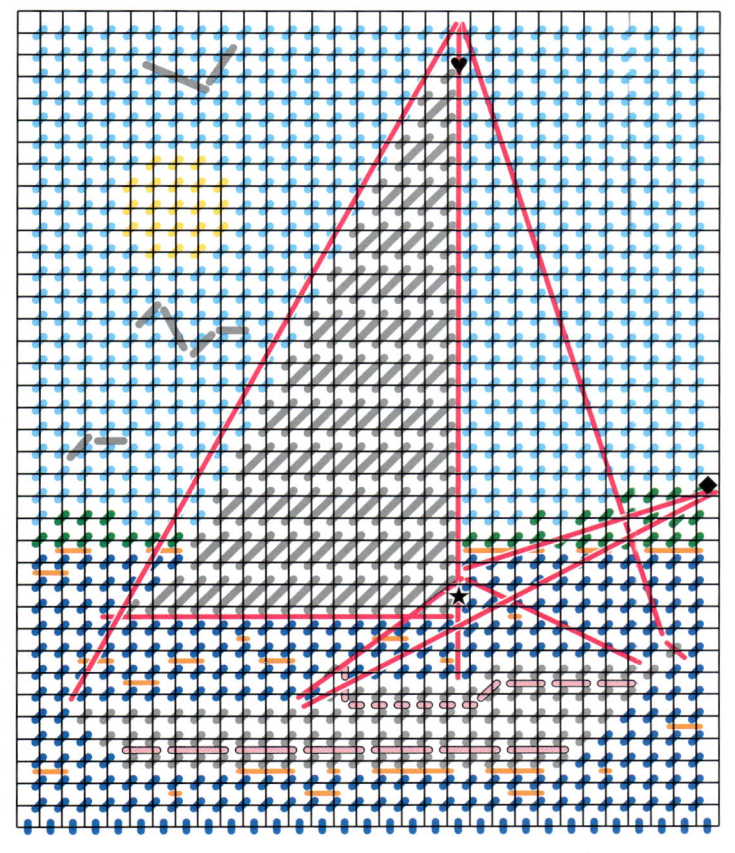

Side #2 (32 x 38 threads) (stitch 2)

Pinwheels Boutique Tissue Box Cover

Size
4 1/2"w x 5 1/2"h x 4 1/2"d
(fits a 4 1/4"w x 5 1/4"h x 4 1/4"d boutique tissue box)

Supplies
Three 10 1/2" x 13 1/2" sheets of 7 mesh plastic canvas
Worsted weight yarn
Four 3/4" paper fasteners
#16 tapestry needle

Stitches Used
Alternating Scotch Stitch, Gobelin Stitch, Overcast Stitch, and Tent Stitch. Refer to **General Instructions**, pages 28-31, for stitch diagrams.

Instructions
Follow charts and photos to cut and stitch tissue box cover pieces, leaving grey shaded areas unworked. Use matching color Overcast Stitches for all joining. Matching long edges, join Sides. Join Top to Sides.

For each Pinwheel, turn Pinwheel piece over. Work stitches in grey shaded areas on wrong side of Pinwheel. With right side up, fold corners of Pinwheel indicated by arrows to center and tack. Insert paper fastener in Pinwheel and Side at ♥. Secure fastener on inside of tissue box cover.

Pastel Color Key	**Bright Color Key**
white	white
lt yellow	yellow
lt pink	orange
lt purple	red
purple	green
lt blue	dk blue
lt green	turquoise

www.leisurearts.com

Pinwheel (30 x 30 threads) (stitch 4)

Side (32 x 38 threads) (stitch 4)

Top (32 x 32 threads)

Forties Flamingos Boutique Tissue Box Cover

Size
4½"w x 5½"h x 4½"d
(fits a 4¼"w x 5¼"h x 4¼"d boutique tissue box)

Supplies
Two 10½" x 13½" sheets of 7 mesh plastic canvas
Worsted weight yarn
Rainbow Gallery metallic blue yarn
Black embroidery floss
#16 tapestry needle

Stitches Used
Alternating Scotch Stitch, Backstitch, Double French Knot, Gobelin Stitch, Overcast Stitch, and Tent Stitch. Refer to **General Instructions**, pages 28-31, for stitch diagrams.

Instructions
Follow charts to cut and stitch tissue box cover pieces. Use matching color Overcast Stitches for all joining. Matching long edges, join Sides. Join Top to Sides.

Color Key
- white
- lt pink
- pink
- lt red
- lavender
- lt blue
- black
- metallic blue
- pink (use 2 plies of yarn)
- green (use 2 plies of yarn)
- black embroidery floss (use 6 strands)
- • pink Double Fr. Knot

Top (32 x 32 threads)

Side #1 (32 x 38 threads) (stitch 2)

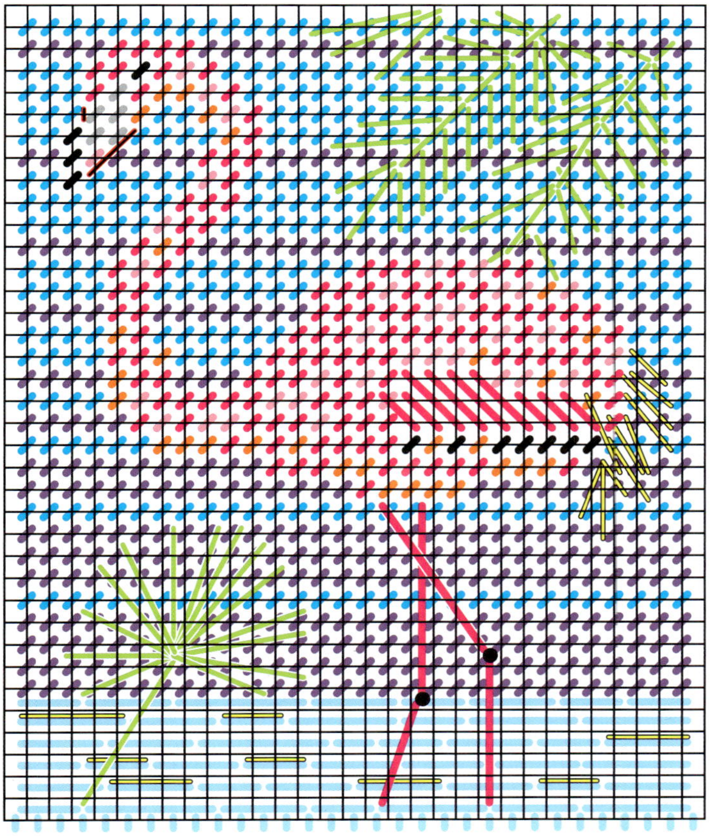

Side #2 (32 x 38 threads) (stitch 2)

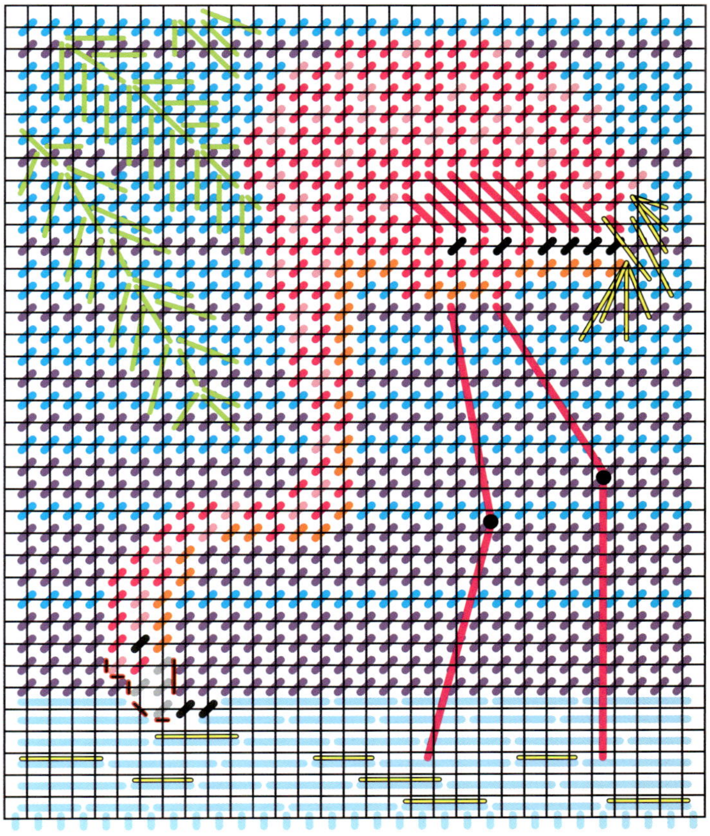

Home Sweet Home Boutique Tissue Box Cover

Size
4 1/2"w x 5 1/2"h x 4 1/2"d
(fits a 4 1/4"w x 5 1/4"h x 4 1/4"d boutique tissue box)

Supplies
Two 10 1/2" x 13 1/2" sheets of 7 mesh plastic canvas
Needleloft® Plastic Canvas Yarn or worsted weight yarn
Embroidery floss
#16 tapestry needle

Stitches Used
Alternating Scotch Stitch, Backstitch, Cross Stitch, Gobelin Stitch, Overcast Stitch, and Tent Stitch. Refer to **General Instructions**, pages 28-31, for stitch diagrams.

Instructions
Follow charts to cut and stitch tissue box cover pieces. Use matching color Overcast Stitches for all joining. Matching long edges, join Sides. Join Top to Sides.

Color Key

Note: Needleloft number is indicated in parentheses.

- white (41)
- yellow (57)
- dk red (03)
- lt blue (35)
- green (27)
- black (00)
- white embroidery floss (use 6 strands)
- brown embroidery floss (use 6 strands)
- black embroidery floss (use 2 strands)
- black embroidery floss (use 6 strands)

Side (32 x 38 threads) (stitch 4)

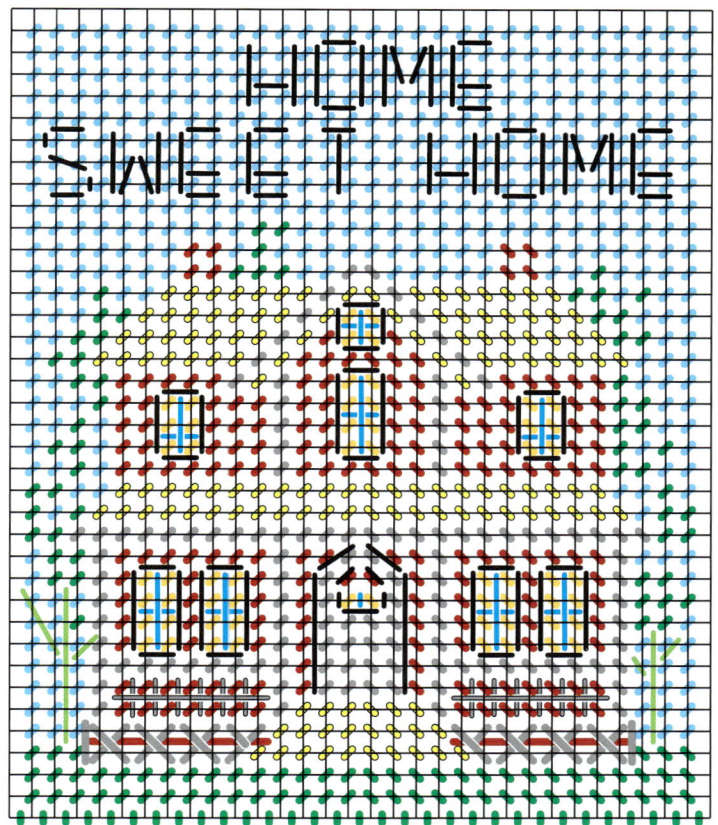

Top (32 x 32 threads)

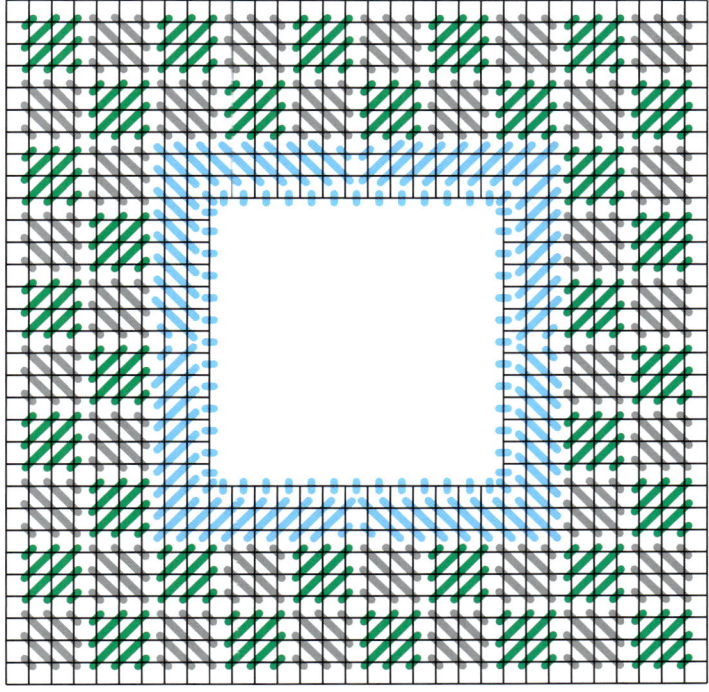

Blue Waves Boutique Tissue Box Cover

Size
4½"w x 5¾"h x 4½"d
(fits a 4¼"w x 5¼"h x 4¼"d boutique tissue box)

Supplies
Two 10½" x 13½" sheets of 10 mesh plastic canvas
Worsted weight yarn
#20 tapestry needle

Stitches Used
Bargello Stitch, Gobelin Stitch, and Overcast Stitch. Refer to **General Instructions**, pages 28-31, for stitch diagrams.

Instructions
Follow charts to cut and stitch tissue box cover pieces. Use black Overcast Stitches to join Sides along long edges. Join Top to Sides.

Top (45 x 45 threads)

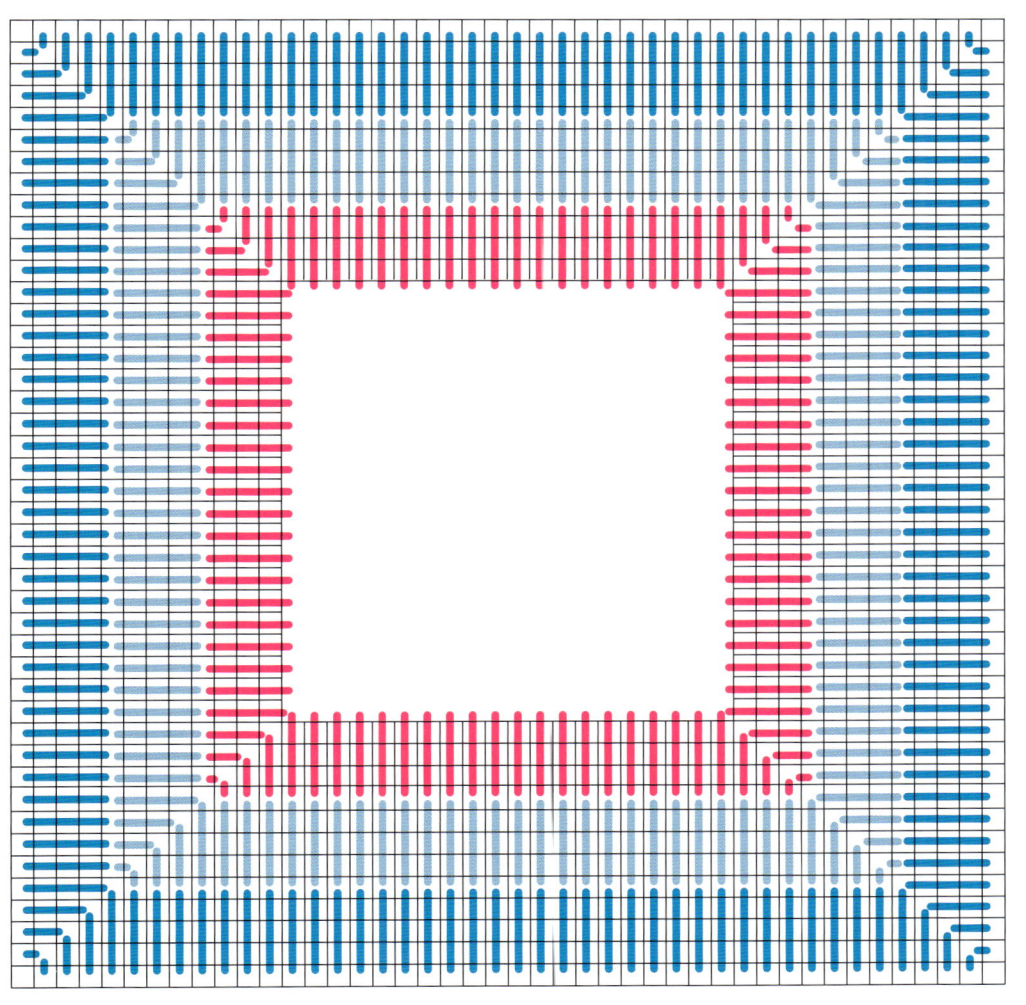

Color Key
- vy lt blue
- lt blue
- blue
- blue-grey
- royal
- dk blue
- black

Continued on page 12.

Blue Waves Boutique Tissue Box Cover
Side (45 x 56 threads) (stitch 4)

Lightning Boutique Tissue Box Cover

Shown on page 10.

Size
4 1/2"w x 5 1/2"h x 4 1/2"d
(fits a 4 1/4"w x 5 1/4"h x 4 1/4"d boutique tissue box)

Supplies
Two 10 1/2" x 13 1/2" sheets of 10 mesh plastic canvas
Worsted weight yarn
#20 tapestry needle

Stitches Used
Bargello Stitch and Overcast Stitch. Refer to **General Instructions**, pages 28-31, for stitch diagrams.

Instructions
Follow charts to cut and stitch tissue box cover pieces. Use vy lt blue Overcast Stitches to join Sides along long edges. Join Top to Sides.

Top (46 x 46 threads)

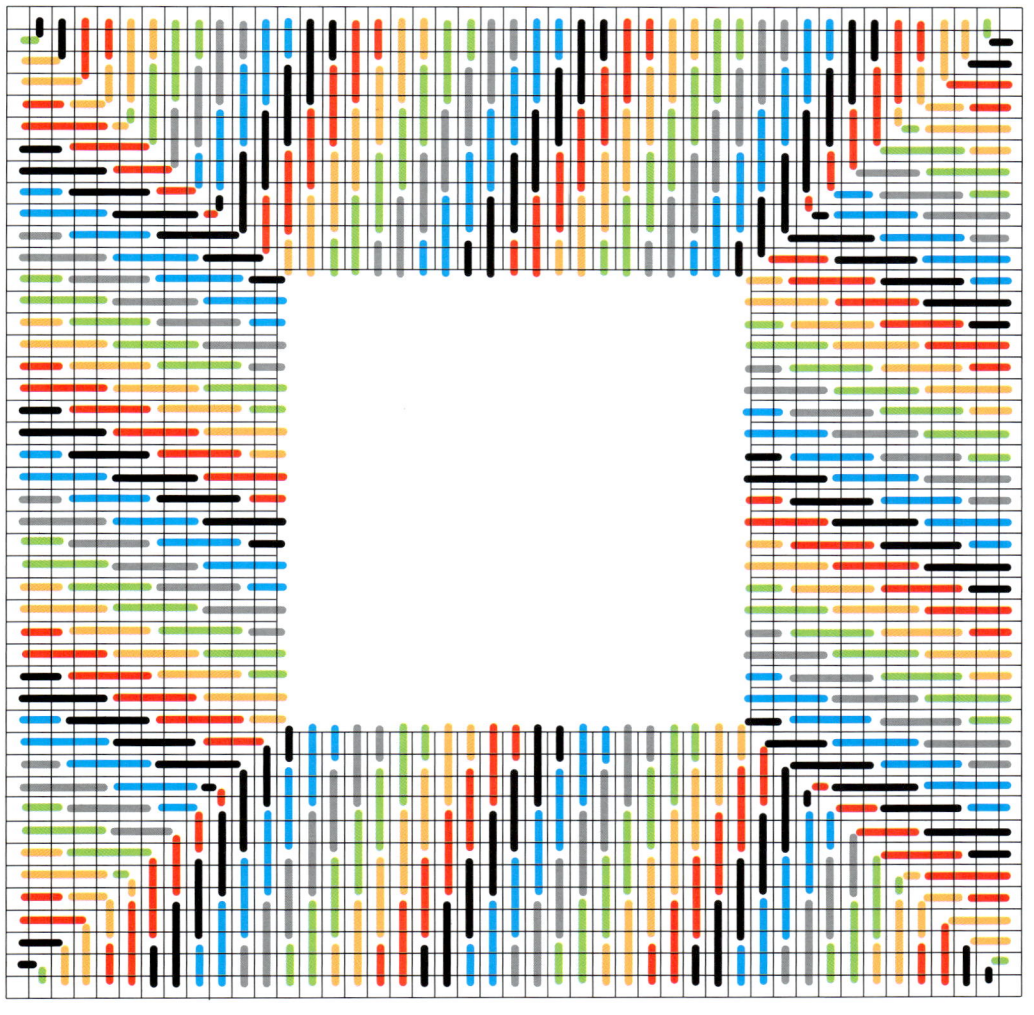

Color Key
- vy lt blue
- lt blue
- blue
- royal
- navy
- black

Continued on page 14.

Lightning Boutique Tissue Box Cover
Side (46 x 55 threads) (stitch 4)

Tulips Boutique Tissue Box Cover

Shown on page 10.

Size
4½"w x 5½"h x 4½"d
(fits a 4¼"w x 5¼"h x 4¼"d boutique tissue box)

Supplies
Two 10½" x 13½" sheets of 10 mesh plastic canvas
Worsted weight yarn
#20 tapestry needle

Stitches Used
Bargello Stitch and Overcast Stitch. Refer to **General Instructions**, pages 28-31, for stitch diagrams.

Instructions
Follow charts to cut and stitch tissue box cover pieces. Use black Overcast Stitches to join Sides along long edges. Join Top to Sides.

Top (46 x 46 threads)

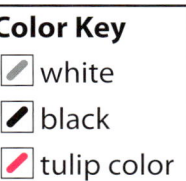

Continued on page 16.

Tulips Boutique Tissue Box Cover
Side (46 x 56 threads) (stitch 4)

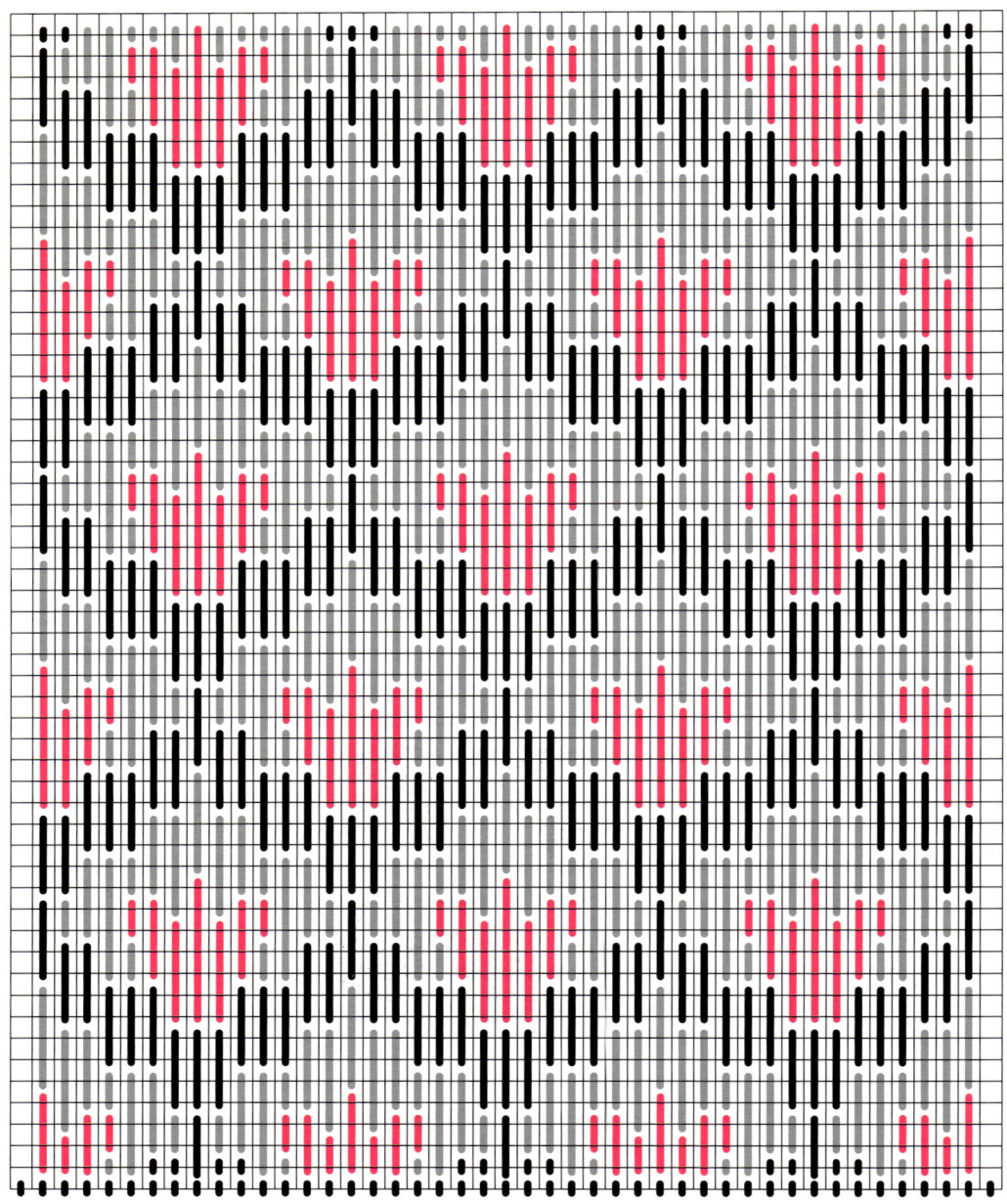

Argyle Family Tissue Box Cover

Shown on page 17.

Size
10"w x 3 3/4"h x 5 1/4"d
(fits a 9 1/2"w x 3 1/2"h x 4 3/4"d tissue box)

Supplies
Two 10 1/2" x 13 1/2" sheets of 7 mesh plastic canvas
Worsted weight yarn
#16 tapestry needle

Stitches Used
Gobelin Stitch, Overcast Stitch, and Tent Stitch. Refer to **General Instructions**, pages 28-31, for stitch diagrams.

Instructions
Follow charts to cut and stitch tissue box cover pieces. Use navy Overcast Stitches for all joining. Matching short edges, join Long Sides to Short Sides. Join Top to Sides. Use navy Overcast Stitches to cover unworked edges.

* Note: for a tissue box measuring 9 1/2"w x 2 1/2"h x 4 3/4"d, cut Short Sides 35 x 19 threads and Long Sides 66 x 19 threads; stitch, omitting border indicated by bracket on charts.

**Short Side (35 x 25 threads)
(stitch 2)**

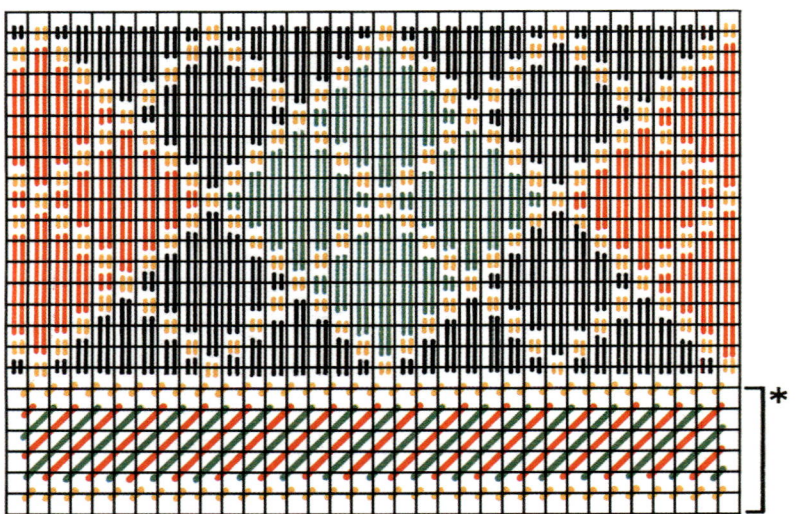

Long Side (66 x 25 threads)
(stitch 2)

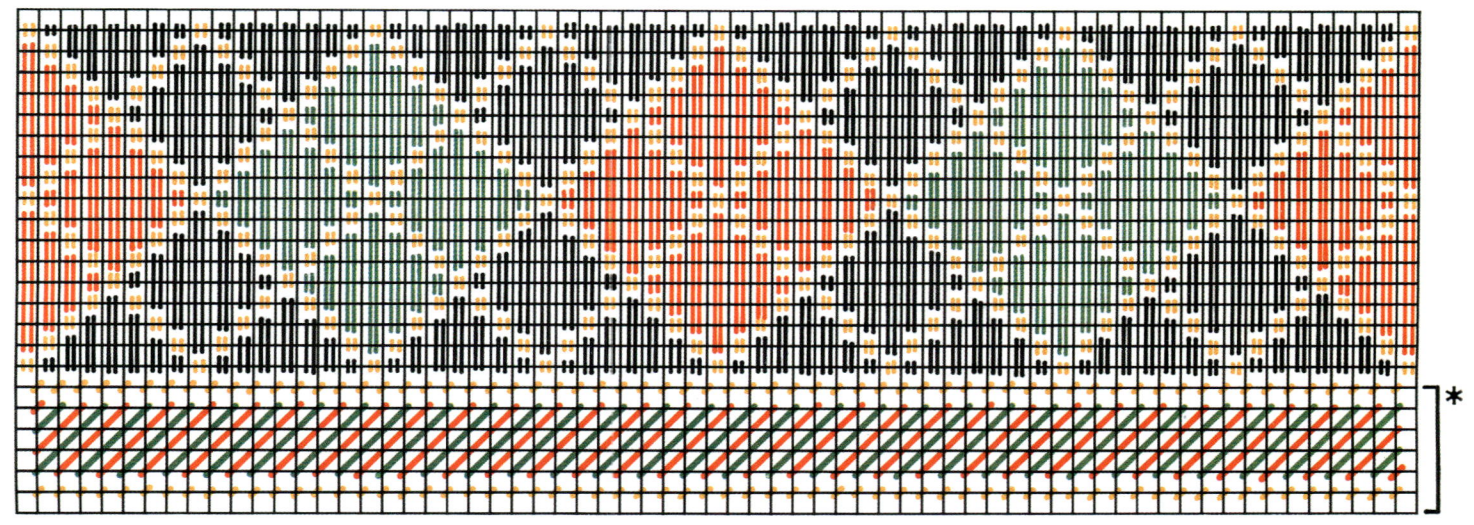

*

Top (66 x 35 threads)

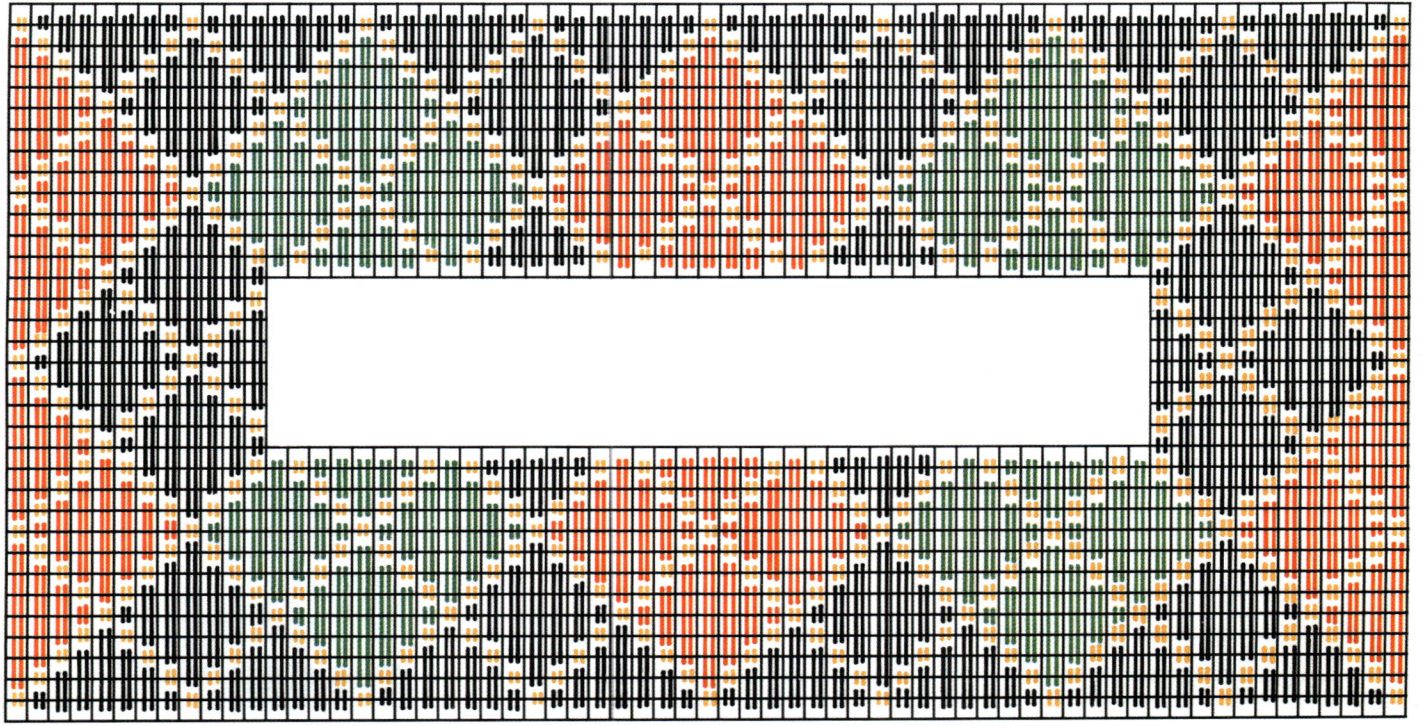

Mushrooms Family Tissue Box Cover

Shown on page 17.

Size
10"w x 3¾"h x 5¼"d
(fits a 9½"w x 3½"h x 4¾"d tissue box)

Supplies
Two 10½" x 13½" sheets of 7 mesh plastic canvas
Worsted weight yarn
#16 tapestry needle

Stitches Used
Mosaic Stitch, Overcast Stitch, and Tent Stitch. Refer to **General Instructions**, pages 28-31, for stitch diagrams.

Instructions
Follow charts to cut and stitch tissue box cover pieces. Use rust Overcast Stitches for all joining. Matching short edges, join Long Sides to Short Sides. Join Top to Sides. Use rust Overcast Stitches to cover unworked edges.

Color Key
- ecru
- lt brown
- rust

*__Note:__ for a tissue box measuring 9½"w x 2½"h x 4¾"d, cut Short Sides 35 x 19 threads and Long Sides 66 x 19 threads; stitch, omitting border indicated by bracket on charts. Work row indicated by ★ using Tent Stitch.

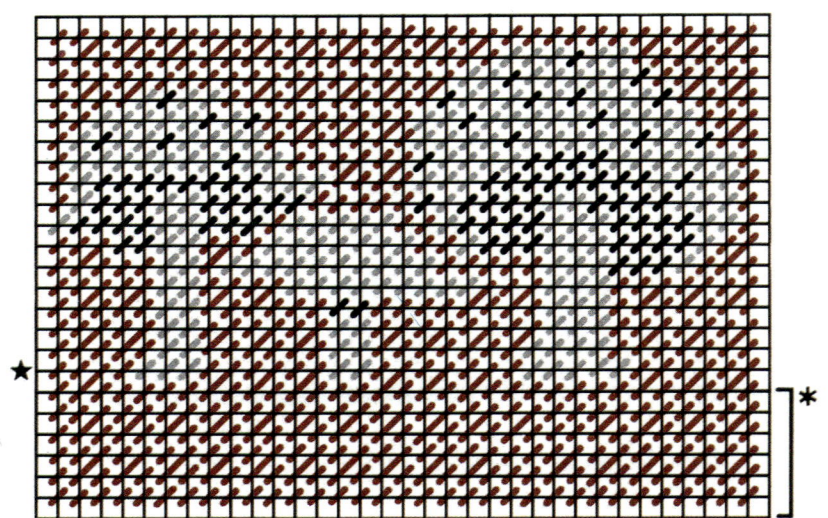

Short Side (35 x 25 threads)
(stitch 2)

Long Side (66 x 25 threads)
(stitch 2)

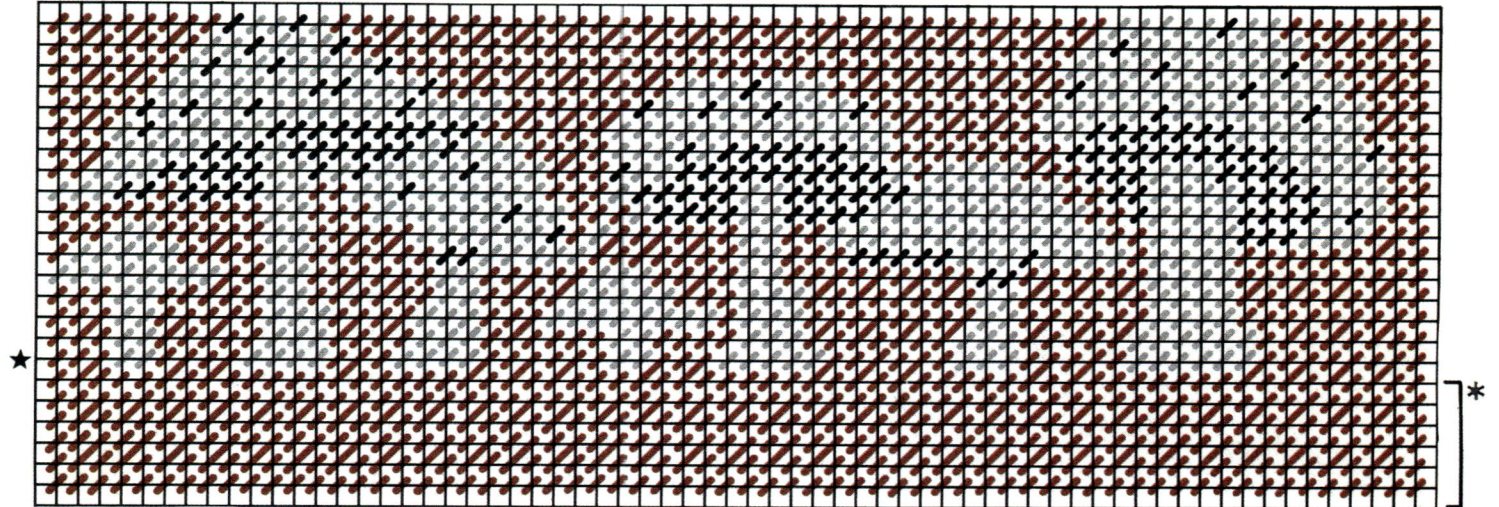

Top (66 x 35 threads)

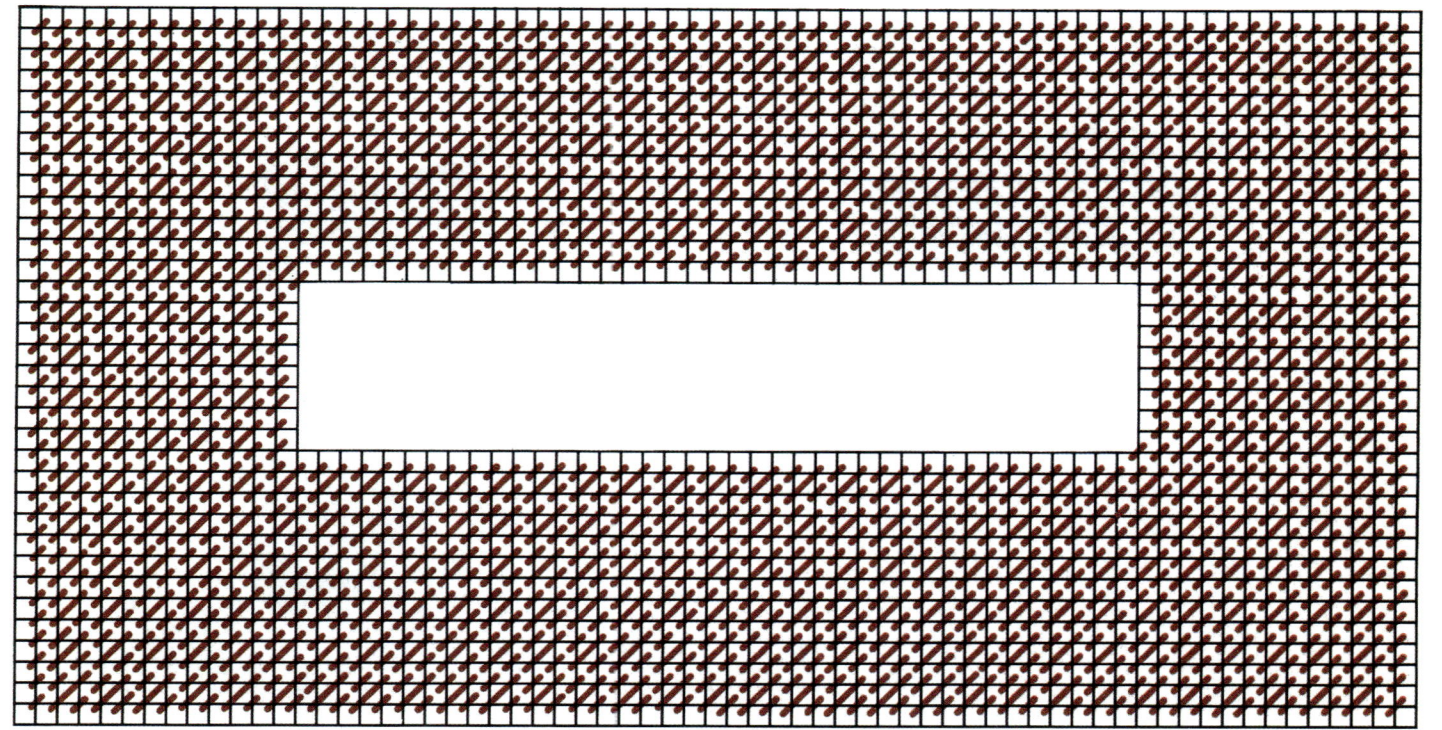

Hearts Boutique Tissue Box Cover

Shown on page 17.

Size
4½"w x 5½"h x 4½"d
(fits a 4¼"w x 5¼"h x 4¼"d boutique tissue box)

Supplies
One 10½" x 13½" sheet of 7 mesh plastic canvas
Worsted weight yarn
#16 tapestry needle

Stitches Used
Gobelin Stitch and Overcast Stitch. Refer to **General Instructions**, pages 28-31, for stitch diagrams.

Instructions
Follow charts to cut and stitch tissue box cover pieces. Stitch Top using white yarn. Use white Overcast Stitches for all joining. Matching long edges, join Sides. Join Top to Sides. Use white Overcast Stitches to cover unworked edges.

Color Key
- white
- lt yellow
- pink
- lavender
- lt blue
- lt green

Top (30 x 30 threads)

Note: Use this chart to complete the top of the Hearts, Zebra, Santa, Kitchen, and Geometric tissue box covers. Refer to instructions and photo for color.

Side (30 x 38 threads)
(stitch 4)

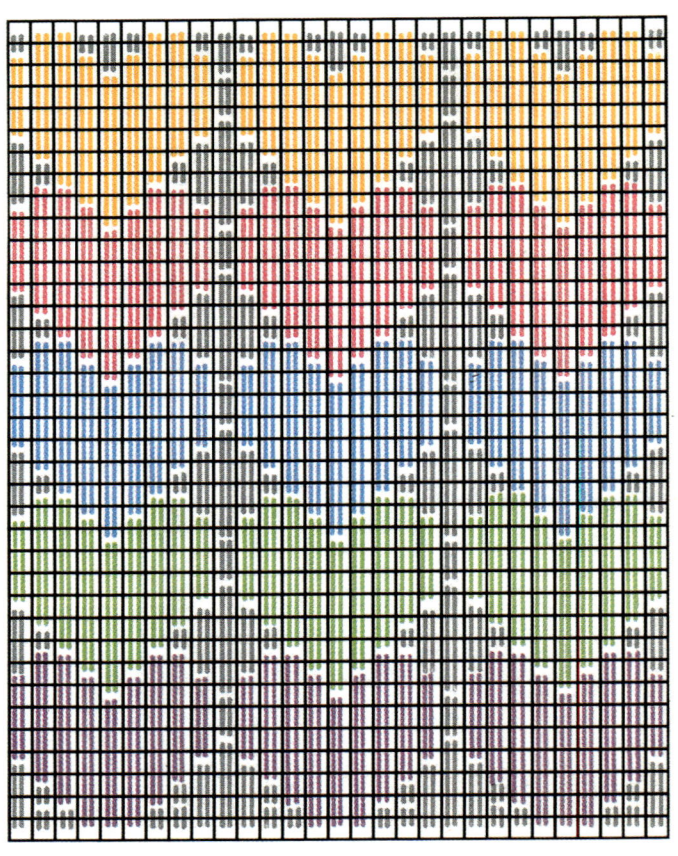

www.leisurearts.com

Zebra Boutique Tissue Box Cover

Shown on page 17.

Size
4½"w x 5½"h x 4½"d
(fits a 4¼"w x 5¼"h x 4¼"d boutique tissue box)

Supplies
One 10½" x 13½" sheet of 7 mesh plastic canvas
Worsted weight yarn
#16 tapestry needle

Stitches Used
Gobelin Stitch, Overcast Stitch, and Tent Stitch. Refer to **General Instructions**, pages 28-31, for stitch diagrams and to make 4 black and white pom-poms.

Instructions
Follow charts to cut and stitch tissue box cover pieces. Stitch Top (chart on page 22) using green yarn. Use green Overcast Stitches for all joining. Matching long edges, join Sides. Join Top to Sides. Use green Overcast Stitches to cover unworked edges.

Color Key
- white
- gold
- green
- brown
- black
- pom-pom placement

Side (30 x 38 threads)
(stitch 4)

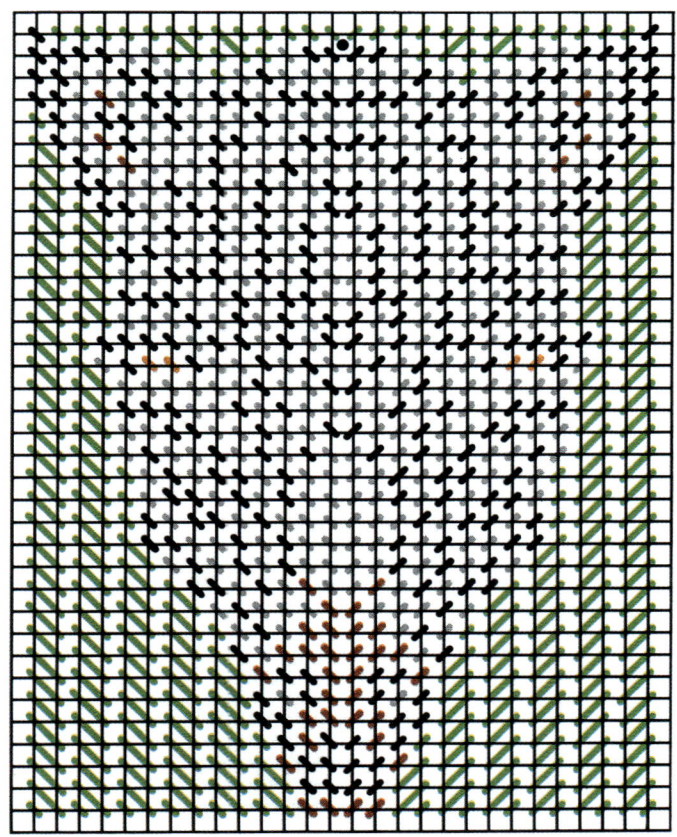

23

Santa Boutique Tissue Box Cover

Shown on page 17.

Size
4 1/2"w x 5 1/2"h x 4 1/2"d
(fits a 4 1/4"w x 5 1/4"h x 4 1/4"d boutique tissue box)

Supplies
One 10 1/2" x 13 1/2" sheet of 7 mesh plastic canvas
Worsted weight yarn
#16 tapestry needle

Stitches Used
Gobelin Stitch, Overcast Stitch, Tent Stitch, and Turkey Loop Stitch. Refer to **General Instructions**, pages 28-31, for stitch diagrams and to make 4 white pom-poms.

Instructions
Follow charts to cut and stitch tissue box cover pieces. Stitch Top (chart on page 22) using dk green yarn. Use dk green Overcast Stitches for all joining. Matching long edges, join Sides. Join Top to Sides. Use dk green Overcast Stitches to cover unworked edges.

Color Key
- white
- lt pink
- pink
- red
- dk green
- black
- white Turkey Loop
- pom-pom placement

Side (30 x 38 threads)
(stitch 4)

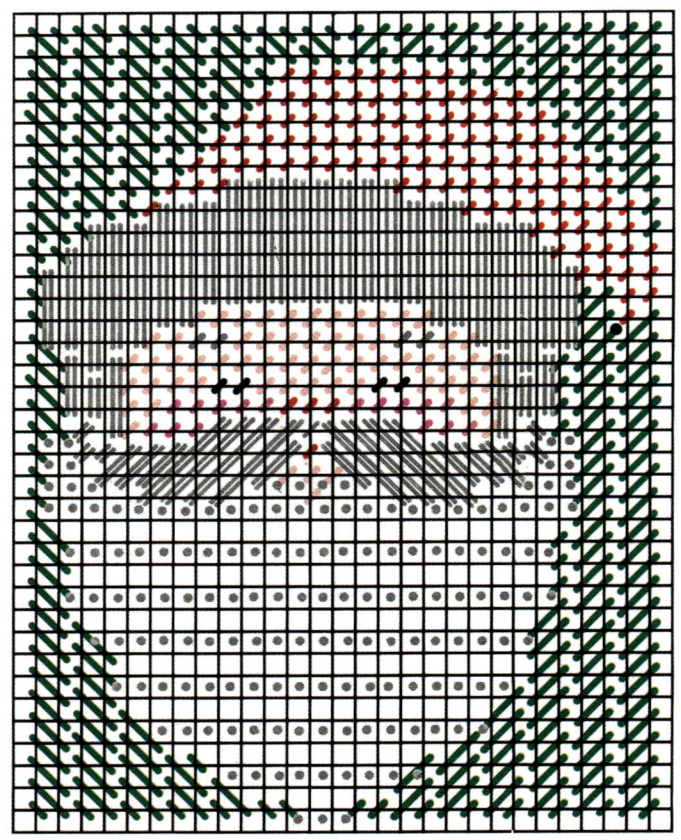

www.leisurearts.com

Kitchen Boutique Tissue Box Cover

Shown on page 17.

Size
4½"w x 5½"h x 4½"d
(fits a 4¼"w x 5¼"h x 4¼"d boutique tissue box)

Supplies
One 10½" x 13½" sheet of 7 mesh plastic canvas
Worsted weight yarn
#16 tapestry needle

Stitches Used
Backstitch, Gobelin Stitch, Overcast Stitch, and Tent Stitch. Refer to **General Instructions**, pages 28-31, for stitch diagrams.

Instructions
Follow charts to cut and stitch tissue box cover pieces. Stitch Top (chart on page 22) using lt yellow yarn. Use lt yellow Overcast Stitches for all joining. Matching long edges, join Sides. Join Top to Sides. Use lt yellow Overcast Stitches to cover unworked edges.

Color Key
- white
- lt yellow
- orange
- pink
- red
- rust
- burgundy
- blue
- lt green
- green
- dk green
- tan
- black

Side (30 x 38 threads)
(stitch 4)

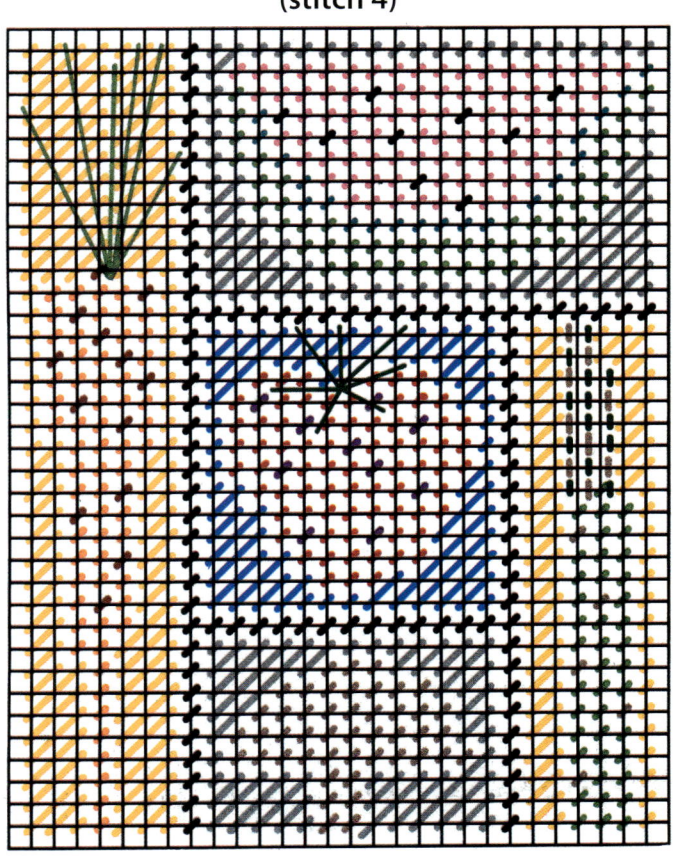

Geometric Boutique Tissue Box Cover

Shown on page 17.

Size
4½"w x 5½"h x 4½"d
(fits a 4¼"w x 5¼"h x 4¼"d boutique tissue box)

Supplies
One 10½" x 13½" sheet of 7 mesh plastic canvas
Worsted weight yarn
#16 tapestry needle

Stitches Used
Gobelin Stitch, Overcast Stitch, and Tent Stitch. Refer to **General Instructions**, pages 28-31, for stitch diagrams.

Instructions
Follow charts to cut and stitch tissue box cover pieces. Stitch Top (chart on page 22) using royal blue yarn. Use royal blue Overcast Stitches for all joining. Matching long edges, join Sides. Join Top to Sides. Use royal blue Overcast Stitches to cover unworked edges.

Color Key
- lt blue
- blue
- royal blue

Side (30 x 38 threads)
(stitch 4)

General Instructions

Working with Plastic Canvas

Counting Threads. The lines of the canvas are referred to as threads. Before cutting out the pieces, note the thread count of each chart listed above the chart, indicating the number of threads in the width and height. To cut plastic canvas pieces accurately, count **threads** (not **holes**) as shown in **Fig. 1**.

Fig. 1

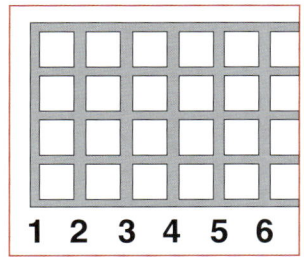

Marking the Canvas. You may use an overhead projector pen to mark the canvas. Outline the shape with pen, cut out, and remove markings before stitching.

Cutting the Canvas. Cut as close to the thread as possible without cutting into the thread. If you don't cut close enough, "nubs" or "pickets" will be left on the edge. Make sure to cut all nubs from the canvas before stitching because nubs will snag the yarn and are difficult to cover. A craft knife is helpful when cutting a small area from the center of a larger piece of canvas. When using a craft knife, protect the table below with a layer of cardboard.

When cutting canvas along a diagonal, cut through the center of each intersection. This will leave enough plastic canvas on both sides of the cut so that both pieces may be used. Properly cut diagonal corners will be less likely to snag yarn and are easier to cover.

Working with Yarn and Floss

Most worsted weight yarn brands have plies which are twisted together to form one strand. When the instructions indicate two plies of yarn, separate the strand of yarn and stitch using only two of the plies. Needleloft Plastic Canvas Yarn is 100% nylon worsted weight yarn suitable for 7 mesh canvas. Embroidery floss is made up of six strands. For smooth coverage, separate and realign the strands before threading your needle.

Reading the Color Key

A color key is included for each project, indicating the color used for each stitch on the chart. Additional information may also be included, such as the number of plies to use when working a particular stitch.

Reading the Chart

When possible, the drawing on the chart looks like the completed stitch. For example, the tent stitches on the chart are drawn diagonally across an intersection of threads just as they look on the piece. When a stitch cannot be clearly drawn on the chart, like a French Knot, a symbol will be used instead.

Stitching the Design

Securing the First and Last Stitches. Don't knot the end of your yarn before you begin stitching. Instead, begin each length of yarn by coming up from the wrong side of the canvas and leaving a 1"-2" tail on the wrong side. Hold this tail against the canvas and work the first few stitches over the tail. When secure, clip the tail close to the stitched piece. Long tails can become tangled in future stitches or can show through to the right side of the canvas. After all the stitches of one color in an area are complete, end by running the needle under several stitches on the back. Trim the end close to the stitched piece.

Using Even Tension. Keep your stitching tension consistent, with each stitch lying flat and even. Pulling or yanking the yarn causes the tension to be too tight, and you will be able to see through your project. If the tension is too loose, the stitches won't lie flat. Most stitches tend to twist yarn. Drop your needle and let the yarn untwist occasionally.

Joining Pieces

Straight Edges. To join two or more pieces along a straight edge, place one piece on top of the other with right or wrong sides together. Make sure the edges are even, then overcast the pieces together through all layers.

Shaded Areas. Shaded areas usually mean that all the stitches in that area are worked on the canvas reverse side or are used to join pieces of canvas. Do not work these stitches until the project instructions say you should.

Tacking. To tack pieces, run your needle under the backs of some stitches on one stitched piece to secure the yarn. Then run the needle through the canvas or under stitches on the piece to be tacked in place. This should securely attach pieces without tacking stitches showing.

Stitch Diagrams

Unless otherwise indicated, bring needle up at **1** and all **odd numbers** and down at **2** and all **even numbers**.

Alternating Scotch Stitch

This Scotch Stitch variation is worked over a number of threads forming alternating blocks as shown in **Fig. 2**.

Fig. 2

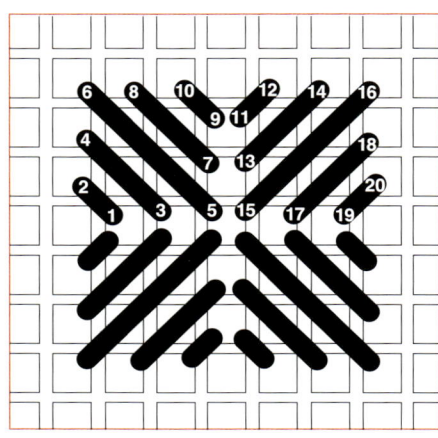

Backstitch

This stitch is worked over completed stitches to outline or define **(Fig. 3)**. It is sometimes worked over more than one thread. It can also be used to cover canvas **(Fig. 4)**.

Fig. 3

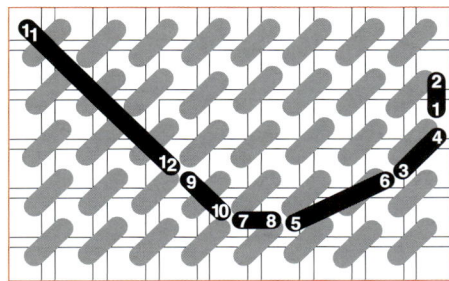

Fig. 4

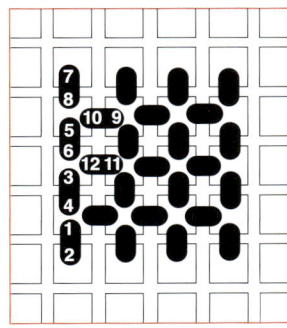

Bargello Stitch

This stitch is a repeated combination of stitches that form a wave pattern. Bargello stitches can be worked either vertically or horizontally and over any number of threads **(Fig. 5)**.

Fig. 5

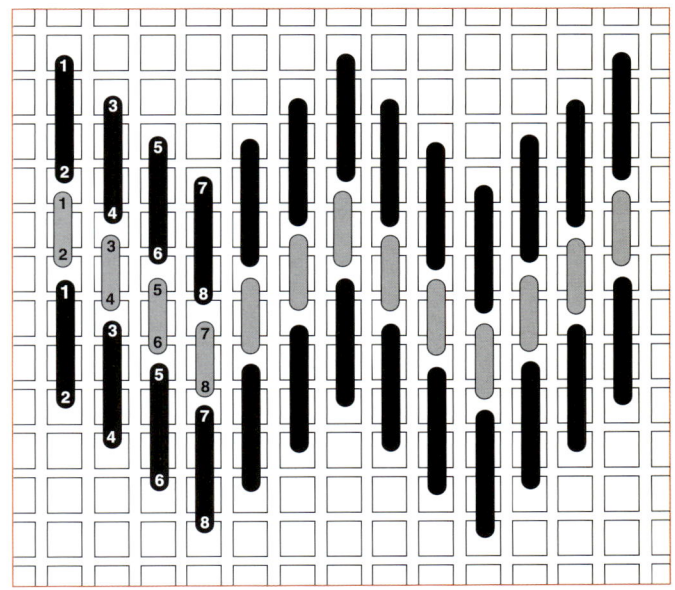

Cross Stitch

This stitch is composed of two stitches **(Fig. 6)**. Cross the top leg of each stitch in the same direction. The number of intersections may vary according to the chart.

Fig. 6

Double French Knot

Bring needle up through hole. Wrap yarn twice around needle and insert needle in same hole, holding end of yarn with non-stitching fingers **(Fig. 7)**. Tighten knot; then pull needle through canvas, holding yarn until it must be released.

Fig. 7

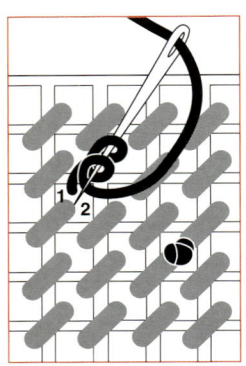

Gobelin Stitch

This straight stitch is worked over two or more threads or intersections **(Fig. 8)**. The number of threads or intersections may vary according to the chart.

Fig. 8

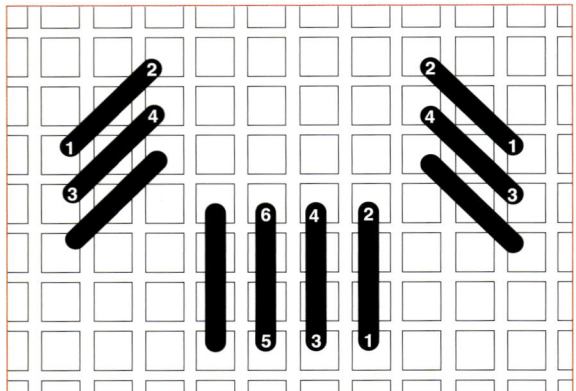

Mosaic Stitch

This three-stitch pattern forms small squares **(Fig. 9)**.

Fig. 9

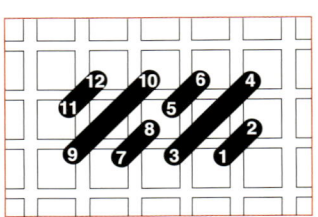

Overcast Stitch

This stitch covers the edge of canvas and joins pieces **(Fig. 10)**. It may be necessary to go through the same hole more than once to get even coverage on the edge, especially at the corners.

Fig. 10

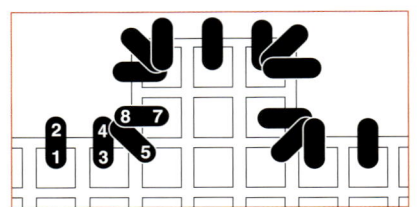

Tent Stitch

This stitch is worked in horizontal or vertical rows over one intersection **(Fig. 11)**. Refer to **Fig. 12** to work the reversed tent stitch.

Fig. 11

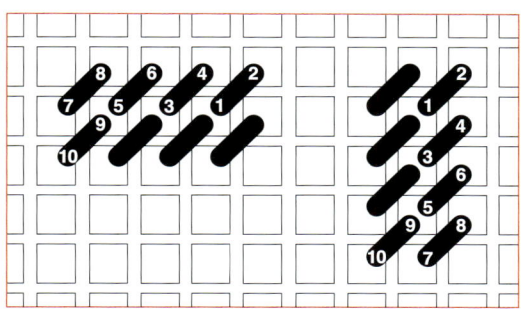

Fig. 12

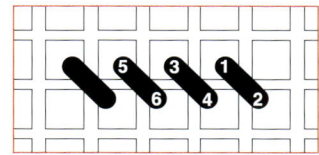

Turkey Loop Stitch

This stitch is composed of locked loops. Bring needle up through hole and back down through same hole, forming a loop on top of the canvas. Make a locking stitch across the thread directly below or to either side of the loop as shown in **Fig. 13**.

Fig. 13

Pom-Pom

Wrap yarn around a 2" length of cardboard 30 times. For Zebra, wrap white yarn 15 times and black yarn 15 times. Carefully slide yarn off cardboard onto flat surface. Knot a single strand of yarn around center of yarn bundle to secure **(Fig. 14)**. Cut yarn loops and trim to form 1½" diameter ball **(Fig. 15)**. Thread ends of yarn used for tying pom-pom through needle and attach.

Fig. 14

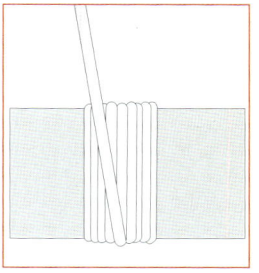

Fig. 15

We have made every effort to ensure that these instructions are accurate and complete. We cannot, however, be responsible for human error, typographical mistakes, or variations in individual work.

Copyright © 2012 by Leisure Arts, Inc., 5701 Ranch Drive, Little Rock, AR 72223. All rights reserved. This publication is protected under federal copyright laws. Reproduction or distribution of this publication or any other Leisure Arts publication, including publications which are out of print, is prohibited unless specifically authorized. This includes, but is not limited to, any form of reproduction or distribution on or through the Internet, including posting, scanning, or e-mail transmission.